HERBS AND SPICES

First published in Great Britain 1983 by
Webb and Bower (Publishers) Limited
9 Colleton Crescent, Exeter, Devon EX2 4BY

Conceived and edited by
the E.T. Archive Limited
Chelsea Wharf, 15 Lots Road, London SW10 0QH

Designed by Julian Holland
Picture Research by Anne-Marie Ehrlich
Copyright © Webb and Bower (Publishers) Limited 1983

British Library Cataloguing in Publication Data

Cockburn, Amy
  Herbs and spices.—(A Webb & Bower Miniature)
  1. Herbs   2. Spices
  I. Title
  641.3'57   SB351.H5

ISBN 0 906671 99 X

Phototypeset by Tradespools Limited, Frome, Somerset
Printed and bound in Hong Kong by Mandarin Offset International Limited

HERBS AND SPICES

Amy Cockburn

Webb&Bower
EXETER, ENGLAND

Angelica

Angelica archangelica

A native of northern Europe, angelica was introduced into Europe in 1568 since when its stem has been highly rated as a medicinal herb. Its properties in healing the plague were said to have been revealed by an angel. The leaves were also eaten after blanching.

Sow seeds in a rich, damp soil in August or in March and pick the flowering and leaf stalks in April or May.

Candied Angelica

Cut the stems into 5in (12cm) sections and put into a pan and cover with boiling syrup. Put a layer of vine or spinach leaves on top and leave for a day. Drain and discard the vine leaves. Boil the syrup and pour over the angelica. Cover with fresh leaves. Repeat this process once more and bottle in airtight jars.

Basil

Ocimum basilicum

Originally from India, basil was introduced to Europe through the monasteries probably around 1548. The Greek name for it meaning royal or king suggests that either it was their most important herb or that it was part of a royal medicine.

Plant seedlings in a warm sheltered position in full sun in June.

Basil is delicious in any tomato dishes as well as in sausages, stuffings and herb butters.

Pistou

large bunch of basil	olive oil
2oz (50g) pine nuts	2 cloves of garlic
1oz (25g) parmesan cheese	salt

Pound the basil, garlic, salt and pine nuts in a mortar or put through a food mill. Add the cheese. When it is a purée, add olive oil and stir constantly until it is the consistency of creamed butter. Serve with pasta or use as flavouring in vegetable soup.

Le Basilic

Ocymum Basilicum, L. C. P.

Bot. Impr. Imprimerie Roy. Basilico Angl. Basil, Esp. Citronea, Basilicon

Bay

Laurus nobilis

A native of southern Europe and cultivated in Britain since the sixteenth century, the Ancients dedicated the bay to Apollo and it was worn as a sign of distinction by military heroes as well as scholars. It is a herb with both healing properties and culinary uses and also has a reputation for warding off lightning and wizards and even today is used to protect cupboards from weevils when it is scattered among flour and spices.

It can be grown as a shrub or tree if protected from frost. The leaves can be picked all the year round and used in *bouquet garnis*, stocks and sparingly in sauces.

Lamb and Bay Leaf Kebabs   Serves 4

1½lb (600g) lamb fillet   olive oil
juice of one lemon   1 medium onion
12 bay leaves

Marinate the lamb chopped into 1in (2½cm) pieces in a little olive oil and lemon juice for one hour. Thread alternate slices of onion, lamb and bay leaf on skewers and grill under a hot fire on all sides for about ten minutes or to taste. Serve with brown rice flavoured with lemon rind and a green salad.

Carle Vernet.   I. lith. de Delpech

Marchand de Lauriers
des lauriers de l'ail.

Caper

Capparis spinosa

The caper is a prickly shrub which, although it grows in many parts of the world, is most popular in western Europe where the fruit is used extensively in making sauces and pickles. It was used medicinally in the fourteenth century, the roots being a preservative for teeth. Pickled capers came into their own around 1480 and by the nineteenth century, a scented tea was made from them.

Poached Meat Balls in Caper Sauce   Serves 4

½oz (15g) butter	2 eggs
2oz (50g) finely chopped onions	½tsp (2.5ml) grated lemon rind salt and pepper
2oz (50g) breadcrumbs	1 onion stuck with cloves
6oz (150g) each of minced beef, pork and veal	3pt (2litre) water
3 anchovies chopped	1 bay leaf and parsley
	2tsp (10ml) capers

Fry onions in butter and mix with bread, mince, anchovies parsley, salt and pepper. Knead thoroughly and shape into eight large meat balls. Poach in water together with onion, bay leaf and salt for 20 minutes. Transfer to heated dish and reserve liquid. For the sauce, make a roux and pour in 1pt (500ml) of the poaching liquid, bring to boil and beat until thick and smooth. Add the lemon rind and capers and stir for 15 minutes. Break the egg yolks into some of the simmering sauce and whisk the mixture back into the pan. Add the meat balls and heat through.

11

Caraway

Carum carvi

A plant that grows wild and is cultivated in Europe, Asia and the USA, it flowers in June and is followed by the brown fruit containing the strongly flavoured seed much used in cakes and breads.

The root is said to have provided the bread for Julius Caesar's army and the seed, together with dill and fennel were given to children to combat hiccups, particularly in Church.

Sow seeds in September or March in fertile, well-drained soil in a sunny position.

Veal with Caraway
Serves 4

1½lb (600g) cubed lean veal	½pt (250ml) chicken stock
2oz (50g) finely chopped onion	4oz (100g) mushrooms
1½oz (4og) butter	salt and pepper
1½tbs (22.5ml) caraway seeds	1oz (25g) plain flour

Sprinkle veal with salt and pepper. Fry the onions in the butter until transparent. Stir in veal cubes, add a little plain flour and the caraway seeds and coat the veal evenly. Cover the pan and cook very gently for ten minutes. Stir in the chicken stock, bring to the boil and reduce to a very low heat. Add mushrooms, cover pan and simmer for one hour or until the veal is tender. Serve with buttered noodles.

Carum Carui.

Drawn by Ingrey & Madeley.

Engraved by W. Smith.

Pub. by Cadlow & Watson, Princes St. Soho, Oct.r 1.st 1828.

13

Chamomile

Matricaria chamomilla

True chamomile is an ancient healing herb used by the Egyptians to cure the ague and by the Greeks in general medicine. It has been used in poultices, in medication to relieve diarrhoea, as a tonic and as a sedative. It is not to be confused with Roman chamomile, *anthemis nobilis*, ideal for making fragrant lawns and the flowers of which can be used as a hair rinse, especially for blond hair. Both herbs are helpful to other plants, particularly in a herb garden and are known to revive drooping leaves if planted nearby.

Sown in sunny well-drained soil in March or April, true chamomile flowers from June to October. Only flowers with very small stalks should be picked and dried as quickly as possible.

Chamomile tea is frequently drunk in France after meals as an aid to digestion and as a sedative for restless babies. It is valuable in facial steam baths both for the skin and against heavy colds.

To make an infusion, allow 2 (5ml) teaspoons of flowers per cup of boiling water and let it stand for 5–10 minutes.

Chives

Allium schoenoprasum

The smallest of the onion tribe, chives originated with the Chinese in 3000 BC. Used in Asia and the Mediterranean in pre-Christian times, they were introduced to Britain by the Romans as 'rush leek'. They have a mild antibiotic effect, are supposed to strengthen the stomach, reduce blood pressure and be beneficial to the kidneys. As a companion to other plants, chives discourage carrot fly, prevent fruit scab and in a strong solution sprayed on gooseberries, prevent mildew.

Sow seeds from September to April in sunny well-drained soil and remove flowers as soon as they appear, to promote the growth of young leaves.

Frankfurter Green Sauce

1 egg yolk	one hard boiled egg chopped
¼pt (125ml) olive oil	1tbs (15ml) chopped chives
1tsp (5ml) lemon juice	1tsp (5ml) chopped parsley and
1tsp (5ml) finely chopped	dill
capers	salt and pepper

Make a mayonnaise with the egg yolk and olive oil. Add while stirring, the lemon juice and a little salt. When mixed, add the remaining ingredients and mix well. Serve as a sauce for cooked potatoes or any white fish.

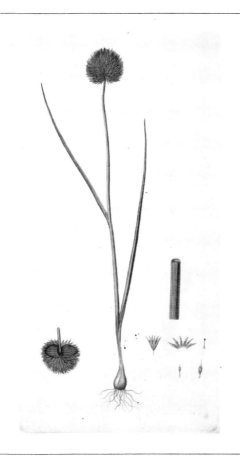

Cinnamon

Cinnamomum zeylanicum

The cinnamon tree is a native of tropical Asia where the bark has long been used as a seasoning. The crusaders brought it to the west and its uses as a flavouring in both sweet and savoury dishes are well known. As a medicine it is a stimulant and a tonic and its oil is also useful as a painkiller for toothache.

Pickled Plums

Makes 1½ pints (750ml)

1lb (500g) small firm plums
1½pt (750ml) distilled white
  vinegar
1½pt (750ml) cold water

1¼lb (600g) sugar
3 whole cloves
½tsp (2.5ml) ground
  cinnamon

Bring ¾pt (375ml) of the vinegar and ¾pt (375ml) of the water to the boil. Pour the liquid over the plums and leave for 1 hour. Pour the liquid back into the pan, reboil and pour over the plums again. Drain the liquid and discard. Put the rest of the liquids into the pan, add the sugar, cloves and cinnamon and bring to the boil stirring to dissolve the sugar. Pour over the plums and let it cool. Pack the plums into a jar, reboil the liquid and pour gently over the plums to ½in (2.5cm) of the top of the jar and seal.

Tab III

Laurus Cinnamomum L.

Dandelion

Taraxacum officinale

The dandelion is a native in Britain, its name coming from *dent de leon* referring to its sharply forked leaves. It has a reputation as an excellent diuretic, thus its name *pissenlit* in France. It is a tonic and a blood purifier. Latex is contained in its roots and the plant itself produces a magenta dye.

Kept in check, seeds can be sown anywhere in the garden, even in full shade. The leaves when picked should be blanched before eating to reduce the bitterness.

Salade de Pissenlits aux Lardons   Serves 4

a large bunch of freshly picked   olive oil
  dandelion leaves   lemon juice
6oz (150g) smoked bacon   salt and pepper
  chopped   4 eggs
4oz (100g) bread in small pieces

Fry the bacon and bread until very crisp. Wash and dry carefully the leaves and mix with bacon and bread. Poach 4 eggs. Make a dressing of the olive oil, lemon juice, salt and pepper and add to the salad. Serve in 4 separate bowls and put in poached egg just before serving.

ichi letician laluraris
tu princripali confir

iquos bias tuas et im
mirertantur
ie de languinibus deus
s mee: et exultabit lin
usticiam tuam
labia mea aperies: et
annuntiabit laudem

n li noluilles lacrifi
sem vtics holocaustis
ibeus
um deo spiritus con
s: cor contritum et hu
deus non despicies

Dens delion.

Fennel

Foeniculum vulgare

This is one of the oldest cultivated herbs, mentioned first in Egyptian papyri and later in Anglo-Saxon herbals as a medicine. Gripe water contains fennel and it is used in compresses, eye washes and expectorants. It was reputed to depress the appetite, thus seeds were eaten in Lent, Fast Days and in Church to reduce hungry cravings.

It is easy to grow simply for its green leaves. However the seeds from the flower heads take a long time to mature. They ripen from September to October and should be dried very slowly.

Trout Flambé   Serves 4

4 medium-sized trout   salt and pepper
2oz (50g) butter   2tbs (30ml) brandy
Bunch of fennel leaves

Clean the trout and put 2–3 fennel stalks into the opening. Place the fish on a bed of fennel branches in an oven-proof dish, cover with melted butter and grill slowly on both sides. When the fish are cooked, take from the grill and pour over the brandy and set it alight. Serve while still burning.

Garlic

Allium sativum

Garlic was known to the Chinese in 2000 BC and its origins in Europe and the Mediterranean go back so far that they cannot be traced. The Greeks bowed down before it and it was both an Egyptian god and part of the diet of the pyramid builders. Believed in many countries to have magic properties, it is reputed still to be useful in the treatment of diarrhoea, ague, rheumatism and high blood-pressure.

To grow garlic, the bulbs should be split into cloves and planted in drills in April or again in October.

Baba ganouge
Serves 4

4 medium-sized aubergines	½tsp (2.5ml) cayenne pepper
4 tomatoes	salt
1 green pepper	4–6 tbs (15ml) olive oil
1 onion	2 lemons
3tsp (15ml) ground cumin	parsley for garnish
2 cloves crushed garlic	

Bake the whole unpeeled aubergines in a moderate oven until very soft. Cool and peel. Chop the flesh coarsely and add the skinned and sliced tomatoes, finely chopped pepper and onion. Mix the spices in a bowl with the oil and lemon juice and add to the aubergine mixture and stir well. Serve with pitta bread and decorate with a little parsley.

Alea.

Lovage

Ligusticum scoticum

Benedictine monks brought this tall perennial herb to northern Europe from the south and from Asia Minor. It is similar to angelica in that the stems can be candied. The seeds are strongly flavoured and were chewed by the Greeks and Romans to aid digestion. It was once thought of as a love potion or aphrodisiac. It is used today as a flavouring in meat dishes and in biscuits.

It is easy to grow by sowing seeds either in September when they are ripe or in the Spring, in a low temperature and in the dark to aid germination. Transplant when large enough to handle.

Lovage Soup
Serves 4

½lb (200g) potatoes diced
1 onion finely chopped
½oz (15g) butter
2pt (1.25litre) stock

2tbs (30ml) fresh chopped
  lovage leaves
parsley
salt and pepper

Fry onion until soft. Add the potatoes and then the lovage. Add the stock, bring to the boil and simmer gently for ½ hour or until the potatoes are soft. Put the soup through a sieve or a blender. Heat and serve sprinkled with chopped parsley.

Flora Danica Tab. CCVII.

Marjoram

Origanum marjorana

Sweet marjoram, called 'Joy of the Mountains' by the Greeks, was brought to England by the Romans who used it to flavour their meat. Along with pot marjoram, *Origanum onites*, and the wild variety *Origanum vulgaris*, it was renowned for its uses in perfumes, nosegays, sweet bags and linens, and the oil was used in ointments and liniments.

Sweet marjoram should be sown in a frost-free and well-protected part of the garden in a medium rich soil.

Pizza alla Napoletana
Serves 4

6oz (125g) plain flour
2oz (50g) butter
1 egg
¼oz (7g) yeast dissolved in water
5–6 fresh tomatoes

6 anchovy fillets
2tsp (5ml) dried marjoram
3oz (75g) mozzarella cheese
olive oil

Make a pastry dough and let it rise for 2 hours. Roll out pastry, cut into two rounds and top with the chopped tomatoes, anchovy fillets and sprinkle with the marjoram. Season sparingly with salt and pepper. Cook the pizza in oiled tins in a hot oven for about 25 minutes. Add the cheese to the pizza about 10 minutes before they are cooked.

Maiorana.

29

Mints

Mentha species

Surely the most common and useful herbs, the mints were important in Egypt, Rome and Greece, not to mention North Africa where its use today in tea is widespread. There are reports of a mint sauce back in the third century and a mint toothpaste in the sixth century. Spearmint, *Mentha viridis*, and apple mint, *Mentha rotundifolia*, are most popular today in cookery. Peppermint, *Mentha piperita*, is used commercially as a flavouring and is also delicious as a tea.

Easy to grow, mints are best planted separately from other herbs. Plant runners in moist rich soil in a sunny position.

Courgettes with Mint   Serves 4

1lb (500g) courgettes cut in slices	salt
2oz (50g) butter	1 large sprig mint finely chopped

Sauté the courgettes in butter and add salt and a little water. Simmer gently with the pan covered for 2–3 minutes. Stir in the mint and continue cooking until tender with the pan uncovered to evaporate the liquid.

Nutmeg

Myristica fragrans

Nutmeg was first imported into Britain by the East India Company in 1769, and the tree which produces it was introduced later by Sir Joseph Banks as a hothouse plant. It was much sought after in the Middle East because of its many properties in medicinal uses and the use of its oil as an opiate. Nutmeg is an aid to digestion and is a mild sedative. In cooking it enhances the flavour of milk dishes but is also delicious in sauces and soups.

The spice is produced from the inner part of the fruit, the outer covering yielding mace. The tree is cultivated in tropical regions but is really only grown successfully in the Moluccas.

Spinach Soup   Serves 4

1lb (500g) leaf spinach   1½ oz (40g) butter
2pt (1.25 litre) ham stock   ½tsp (2.5ml) nutmeg
1½oz (40g) plain flour   salt and pepper

Wash spinach and discard tough stalks. Add to the stock, bring to the boil and simmer for 2–3 minutes. Make a roux from the butter and flour, add a little stock and return it to the spinach and cook for 5 minutes stirring frequently. Put the soup through a sieve or a blender. Reheat and add the nutmeg and season with salt and pepper, but be sparing with the salt. Serve garnished with a little sour cream.

Parsley

Petroselinum crispum

This hardy biennial is the most useful herb in the garden. It was dedicated to Persephone by the ancient Greeks whose athletes were crowned with parsley chaplets and tombs decorated with parsley garlands, which probably contributed to the superstition that to transplant young plants is unlucky. A native of northern and central Europe, it was introduced into England in about 1550. The oil, apiol, has given it a reputation as a useful medicine and it is used today in 'natural' dog rearing medically and as a tonic.

Although it is classed as a biennial, it is best to sow fresh seeds each year in a rich well-worked soil. Keep well watered and weedfree.

Tabbouleh   Crushed wheat, mint and parsley salad
Serves 4–6

3¼oz (75g) fine burghul (crushed wheat)
3 tomatoes finely chopped
6tbs (15ml) chopped parsley
4oz (100g) chopped onion

4tbs (60ml) fresh lemon juice
1½tsp (7.5ml) salt
4tbs (60ml) olive oil
2tbs (30ml) chopped mint
cos lettuce leaves

Put burghul in a bowl and add enough cold water to cover it. Leave for 10 minutes. Drain carefully, wrap in cheese-cloth and squeeze dry. Replace wheat in the bowl with the tomatoes, parsley, mint, onions, lemon, salt and pepper and mix carefully. Test for seasoning. Add the olive oil at the last minute and serve on the lettuce leaves.

Apium Petroselinum.

Published by W. Woodville. March 1. 1791.

Pepper

Piper nigrum

Black pepper, a climbing vine, is grown in the tropics of Asia, originating in eastern India. It is one of the oldest spices to be imported from the East, the Romans using it both in cooking and in medicine. An antiseptic, it was used for healing wounds and to help sufferers from diarrhoea, gout, smallpox and other ailments.

The spice comes from unripe berries picked and dried immediately. If the unripe berries are pickled in vinegar, they are called green pepper and have their own special flavour.

Fillet Steak au Poivre Vert   Serves 2

2 thick slices fillet steak	4tbs (15ml) veal stock
olive oil	1 tomato
3tbs (45ml) red wine vinegar	2tbs (30ml) cream
6tbs (90ml) red wine	15 green peppercorns

Brush meat with the oil and cook on both sides over a high heat, according to taste. Transfer to a heated dish. Deglaze the pan with the vinegar and wine and reduce. Add the stock, tomato and peppercorns and boil rapidly. Reduce the heat and add the cream. Pour over the steaks and serve immediately.

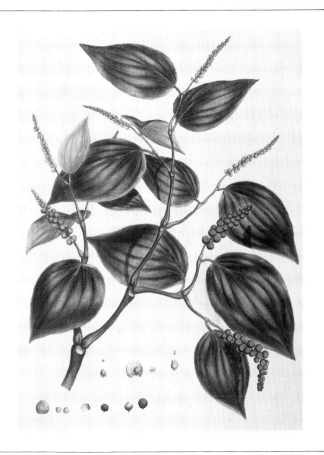

Rosemary

Rosmarinus officinalis

Shakespeare's Ophelia says, 'there's rosemary for remembrance', and the Greeks before that prized this herb for its powers to stimulate the brain. It was a popular stillroom and kitchen herb in the Middle Ages and is said to help stimulate the appetite, aid the circulation of the blood and strengthen the nervous system.

Plant cuttings in a sunny well-drained position sheltered from strong winds and from frost.

Grilled Poussin and Rosemary

Serves 4

2 poussins
4 sprigs rosemary

salt and pepper
olive oil

Split the poussins along the base, spread out the 2 sides using the backbone as a hinge. Flatten the poussins and secure the sides with a skewer. Marinate the birds in the olive oil seasoned with salt and pepper and the rosemary for at least 1 hour. Remove from the marinade and grill each side starting with the underside for about 15 minutes or until they are cooked and are nicely browned. Baste frequently with the marinade mixture. Cut each poussin into 2 along the backbone and serve with a green salad.

Rosmarinus officinalis

Sage

Salvia officinalis

A hardy, evergreen shrub, sage is one of the most important medical herbs in history. It was supposed to cure a quantity of diseases in the Middle Ages and the juice from its leaves was drunk to combat the plague. Sage tea was very common and an infusion of the leaves was taken for colds and chest complaints.

Plant cuttings in March and April in a sunny well-drained site. The flowers appear in June, July and August, but the leaves can be picked almost all the year in a mild climate.

Saltimbocca alla Romana
Serves 4

8 very small veal *escalopes*
8 small slices Parma ham
8 sage leaves

2tbs (30ml) dry white wine
salt and pepper

Sandwich the sage leaves between a slice of ham and the veal and secure with a toothpick. Fry both sides quickly in butter. Season with a little salt and pepper and moisten with the wine. Serve hot on a serving dish with the sauce poured over.

41

Summer Savory

Satureia hortensis

Summer savory was widely used in Roman cooking and was brought to Britain during the Caesars, achieving great popularity under the Saxons. It reached the USA with the first English settlers in the early seventeenth century. It contains a volatile oil and is sometimes used as a digestive medicine, but it is more useful as an aromatic herb as an alternative to pepper.

Seeds should be sown in full sun in a rich soil in April or May and leaves picked before it flowers in June or July.

Broad Beans with Bacon

Serves 4–6

1lb (500g) shelled broad beans
¼lb (100g) unsmoked bacon diced
1 small onion finely chopped

½pt (250ml) chicken stock
2tsp (5ml) chopped savory
salt and pepper ·

Sauté the bacon until crisp and drain. Add the onions and sauté until transparent. Add the beans. Pour the stock over the beans until they are just covered. Add the savory and simmer gently until the beans are just cooked. Remove lid towards the end of cooking to evaporate surplus liquid and add a little butter to glaze.

atia et trmor: tanta su
n contritione et amor:
oposito et humilitate s
xdit saluti anime mee.
ichi queso illius domini
is non solum suscipere sa
itum sz et effectum sacu
Omntissime domine dc
chi suscipere corpus vm
tu domini nostri iesu
od traxit de virgine ma
corpori suo mistico me(r)
xporari ac inter sancta
membra salubriter conu
i. O pater amantissime
e michi dilectum filium
quem nunc quidem de

Carnete.

Tarragon

Artemisia dracunculus

Russian and French tarragon are the culinary herbs cultivated today and they are indigenous to the south-east of
the USSR and central Asia. The herb is a digestive and a
carminative and its oil is used in perfumery.

Plant cuttings in October or March in a sunny,
sheltered position in well-drained soil and harvest leaves
just before flowering.

Rognon de Veau Printanier   Serves 4

2 veal kidneys trimmed but   2tbs (30ml) chopped parsley,
   surrounded by their fat   chervil and tarragon
2 sprigs fresh tarragon   1tbs (15ml) Dijon mustard
2 sprigs fresh parsley   2tbs (30ml) butter
4floz (1dl) dry white wine   salt and pepper

Brown the kidneys all over in their fat. Add the tarragon
and parsley and cook uncovered for 20 minutes. Add salt
and pepper. Remove kidneys from the pan and keep
warm. Deglaze the juices in the pan with the wine, add the
chopped herbs and reduce until nearly dry. Beat in the
mustard and then the butter in small pieces to thicken the
sauce. Check seasoning. Remove the fat from the kidneys
and replace them in the pan in the sauce and heat gently.
Serve sliced accompanied by new potatoes.

Artemisia dracunculus. L.

Thyme

Thymus vulgaris

Used by the ancient Greeks, thyme was brought to England by the Romans becoming so widely used that by the sixteenth century it was under extensive cultivation. Thyme soup was thought to help overcome shyness and the plant itself was used as an antiseptic and in the treatment of throat and chest infections.

Sown in drills in a dry well-drained sunny position, thyme is happiest in rock-gardens.

Sauté de lapin au vin blanc

Serves 4

The marinade

3tbs (45ml) dry white wine
2tbs (30ml) white wine vinegar
2tbs (30ml) olive oil
1 onion finely chopped
½tsp (2.5ml) dried thyme
1 bay leaf
2tsp (10ml) chopped parsley

2½–3lb (1.5kg) fresh rabbit jointed
12–16 peeled small onions
1 clove garlic
¼lb (100g) salt pork diced
3 shallots
¼pt (125ml) chicken stock
½oz (15g) plain flour

Marinate the rabbit pieces for 8 hours. Preheat oven to Gas Mark 4/350°F/180°C. Sauté pork dice and remove from pan. Brown the onions and remove. Take rabbit from marinade, dry well, then brown all over and transfer to casserole. Sauté shallots and garlic, stir in flour and cook gently. Add stock and let sauce thicken. Pour over rabbit, add reserved marinade and cook in oven for 40 minutes. Add small onions and cook for a further 20 minutes.

Thymus Serpyllum.

Sources and Acknowledgements

5. Angelica, J. Roques, *Phyographie Médicale*, 1821
7. Basil, F. and C. Regnault, *La Botanique mise a la portée de tout le monde*, 1774
9. Bay, engraving by Delpech, nineteenth century
11. Caper, watercolour from *Flora of India*, nineteenth century
13. Caraway, *Flora Medica*, 1829
15. Chamomile, Jean de Bourdichon's *Hours of Anne of Burgundy* manuscript sixteenth century (Bibliothèque Nationale)
17. Chives, G.C. Oeder, *Flora Danica*, 1799
19. Cinnamon, Daniel Wagner, *Pharmaceutisch*, 1828
21. Dandelion, Jean de Bourdichon's *Hours of Anne of Burgundy*, manuscript sixteenth century (Bibliothèque Nationale)
23. Fennel, John Miller, *Insects and Plants*, 1780
25. Garlic, *Tacuinum Sanitatum*, 1385 (Bibliothèque Nationale)
27. Lovage, G.C. Oeder, *Flora Danica*, 1799
29. Marjoram, *Tacuinum Sanitatum*, 1385 (Bibliothèque Nationale)
31. Mint, J. Sowerby and J.E. Smith, *English Botany, 1802* (Linnean Society)
33. Nutmeg, Elizabeth Twining, *The Natural Order of Plants*, 1855
25. Parsley, William Woodville, *Medical Botany*, 1832
37. Pepper, watercolour by John Miller (Victoria and Albert Museum)
39. Rosemary, J. Sibthorpe, *Flora Graeca*, 1802
41. Sage, *Tacuinum Sanitatum*, 1385 (Bibliothèque Nationale)
43. Savoury, Jean de Bourdichon's *Hours of Anne of Burgundy*, manuscript, sixteenth century (Bibliothèque Nationale)
45. Tarragon, P.J. Bergius, *Materia Medica*, 1778
47. Thyme, William Curtis, *Flora Londinensis*, 1817

Title page: Fennel, T. Sheldrake, *Botanicum Medicinale*, 1759

The photographs were taken by Eileen Tweedy.

The publishers would like to thank the staff of the library at the Royal Botanic Gardens, Kew for their help.